Unemployment Insurance: Reinsurance and Cost Equalization Proposals

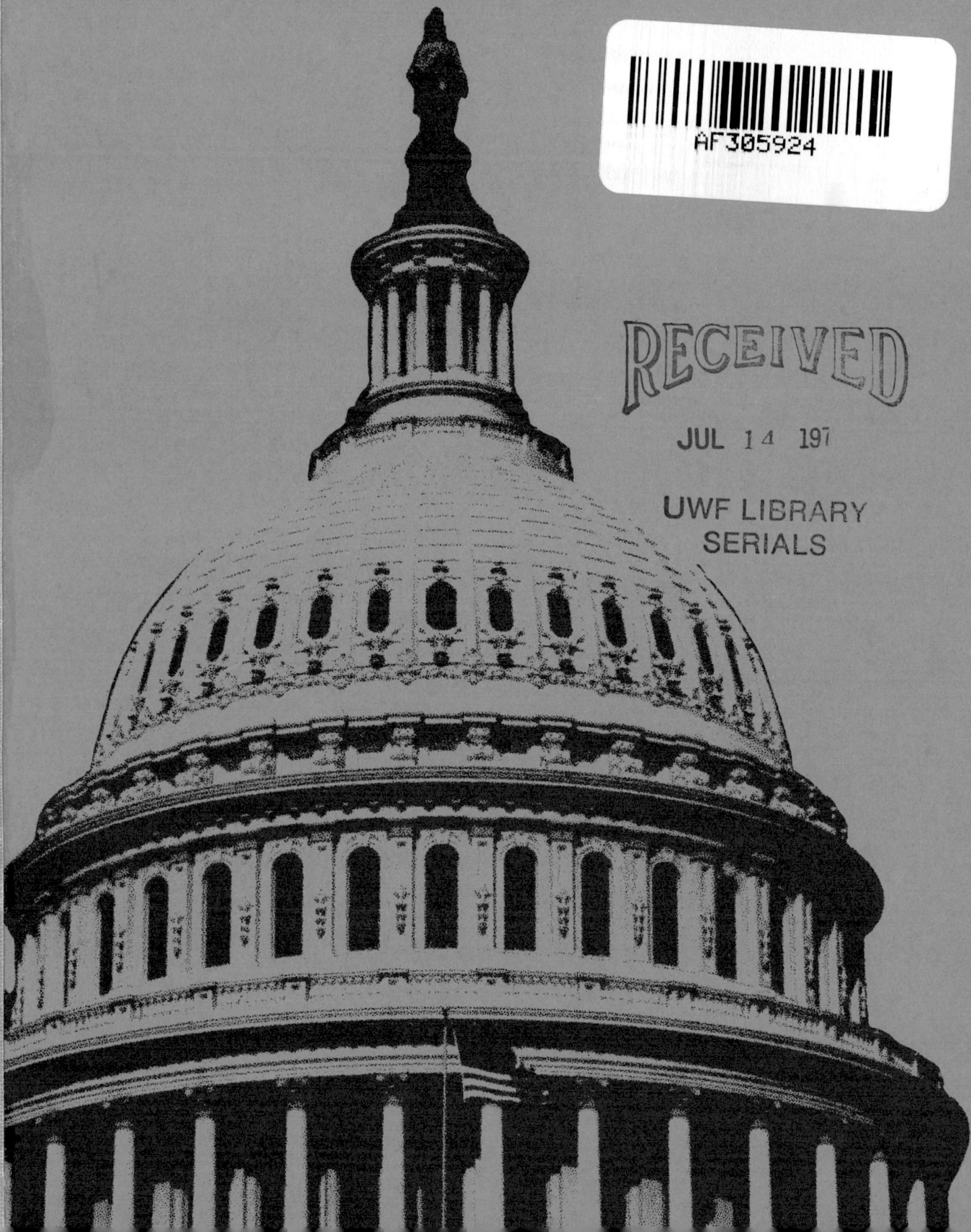

Unemployment Insurance: Reinsurance and Cost Equalization Proposals

American Enterprise Institute for Public Policy Research
Washington, D.C.

ISBN 0-8447-0212-9
Legislative Analysis No. 30, 95th Congress

20 June 1978

Price $2.00 per copy

CONTENTS

INTRODUCTION

The unemployment insurance program is a federal-state program that provides workers who are temporarily unemployed with an income to help them meet their living expenses.[1] The program involves both the collection of money to finance the program and the payment of benefits. This analysis of two pending bills (S. 1853 introduced by Senator Jacob Javits [R-N.Y.] and seven cosponsors, and H.R. 8292 introduced by Representative William M. Brodhead [D-Mich.] and seven cosponsors) is limited to the financing of the program.[2] Financing in turn involves both the size of the total tax burden and the distribution of the tax burden. This analysis is concerned only with the distribution of the burden of taxation.

Currently, the cost of the unemployment insurance program is financed by two taxes. The states levy taxes of varying rates on employers. These taxes pay the cost of most of the benefits payable under the program and all of the regular unemployment insurance benefits. The federal government levies a tax on employers to pay for various administrative costs (including those of state agencies).[3] In addition, the federal tax pays the federal share of the extended and emergency unemployment insurance programs[4] and allocations to a loan fund from which states may borrow if they have temporary cash shortages.

Some states have substantially higher unemployment rates than others. The financing provisions of the bills discussed in this analysis would provide a federal subsidy, out of general revenues, for states with unusually high rates of unemployment. For the future, the bills would permanently modify the financing structure of the unemployment insurance program. But both bills also look to the past and would apply the subsidy retroactively to cover certain past deficits in state financing. Although the retroactive and prospective features are combined in the bills, a choice can be made to adopt only one or the other feature or neither.

THE CURRENT FINANCING DILEMMA

Unemployment experience in recent years has caused heavy state borrowing from the federal unemployment insurance account. If the states are to repay these loans and build adequate reserves in their unemployment insurance trust fund accounts to meet future needs, many states will have to increase significantly the burden of state payroll taxes on employers.

Scope and Magnitude of the Dilemma

The condition of state unemployment insurance trust funds as of June 1977 is shown in Table 1. The bills under consideration attempt to deal with low and, in several cases, negative reserves. The right-hand column of the table shows the average tax rate which each state would have to levy on its employers during the five-year period from 1978 through 1982 to restore adequate reserves to its fund by the end of the period.[5]

Table 1 is based on two assumptions—that total payrolls will increase 6 percent annually in each state, and that each year's benefit-cost rate will equal the state's average cost rate during the ten-year period 1967–1976. (The benefit-cost rate is the ratio of benefits to wages, usually total wages, over a certain time, usually a year.) The validity of these assumptions will vary, of course, with the individual states. In general, the assumption that total payrolls will increase 6 percent annually is probably on the conservative side, perhaps reflecting New York's below average experience. New Jersey, for example, experienced a growth in payrolls of almost 9 percent during the 1967–1975 period.

The assumption that the states must pay off their debts to the federal unemployment insurance account by 1982 is also on the conservative side. In fact, the states do not have to begin repayment until 1981 and do not have to complete repayment for some years thereafter.

Current estimates by the Unemployment Insurance Service of the Department of Labor indicate that by 1981, barring a serious economic recession, practically all the states will have accumulated substantial reserves. Thus, Table 1 probably overstates the magnitude of the financial dilemma.

On the other hand, the required tax rates shown in Table 1 are in terms of total wages rather than taxable wages. If these rates were related directly to taxable wages, they would need to be about double those shown. The ratio

Table 1
**Average Tax Rate Required during Period 1978–1982 to Raise
Reserves to Adequate Level by 1982**

State	Reserves Excluding Loans as of June 1977 (millions of dollars)	Average Required Tax Rate[a]
United States	435.2	1.8
Alabama	− 33.5	1.7
Alaska	76.6	2.6
Arizona	46.2	1.4
Arkansas	− 17.0	2.0
California	823.2	2.0
Colorado	42.8	0.7
Connecticut	− 377.4	3.4
Delaware	− 6.3	2.0
District of Columbia	− 41.4	1.7
Florida	77.3	1.1
Georgia	221.1	1.0
Hawaii	− 8.1	2.2
Idaho	51.8	1.3
Illinois	− 614.9	1.6
Indiana	230.5	0.9
Iowa	42.3	1.1
Kansas	146.5	0.8
Kentucky	127.0	1.5
Louisiana	142.9	1.3
Maine	− 19.7	2.5
Maryland	− 8.7	1.6
Massachusetts	− 164.4	2.9
Michigan	− 319.4	2.7
Minnesota	− 121.3	1.7
Mississippi	106.7	0.7
Missouri	98.4	1.3
Montana	− 3.9	2.2
Nebraska	45.1	0.9
Nevada	7.6	2.3
New Hampshire	33.9	1.3
New Jersey	− 551.9	3.3
New Mexico	31.5	1.2
New York	− 71.7	2.1
North Carolina	238.8	1.2
North Dakota	14.1	1.4
Ohio	198.6	1.4
Oklahoma	29.5	1.0
Oregon	47.6	2.0
Pennsylvania	− 746.4	2.6
Rhode Island	− 63.4	3.8
South Carolina	80.4	1.5
South Dakota	12.3	0.6
Tennessee	156.5	1.2
Texas	223.6	0.5
Utah	20.3	1.4
Vermont	− 42.3	3.2

Table 1 (continued)

State	Reserves Excluding Loans as of June 1977 (millions of dollars)	Average Required Tax Rate[a]
Virginia	80.9	0.7
Washington	− 87.6	3.1
West Virginia	81.9	1.3
Wisconsin	180.3	1.5
Wyoming	38.4	0.6

[a] Tax as percent of total payrolls.

Note: The adequate level is assumed to be 1.5 times the highest annual benefit-cost rate during most recent ten years. Assumptions underlying calculations of tax rates are: (1) total payrolls increase 6 percent annually in each state; and (2) each year's benefit-cost rate equals the state's average cost rate for the period 1967–1976.

Source: Table prepared for Interstate Conference of Employment Security Agencies by Murray Dorkin, New York State Department of Labor, 1977.

of taxable wages to total wages varies from state to state. Total wages were used here because they provide a better basis for interstate comparisons and a better measure of the economic burden.

As shown by Table 1, the fiscal burden that employers must carry varies greatly among states. Five states (Connecticut, New Jersey, Rhode Island, Vermont, and Washington) would have to impose an average tax of over 3 percent of total payrolls. At the other extreme, nine states (Colorado, Indiana, Kansas, Mississippi, Nebraska, South Dakota, Texas, Virginia, and Wyoming) would have to impose an average tax of less than 1 percent of total payrolls. The average required tax would be between 2 and 3 percent of total payrolls for thirteen states, and between 1 and 2 percent for twenty-three states.

These are average rates for unemployment insurance taxes payable over a five-year period. If a state imposed a uniform rate on all its employers, the rate stated in Table 1 is the rate that each employer would have to pay in each of the five years. If a state wished to maintain rates proportional to each employer's own experience with unemployment, then to the extent that some employers were taxed at a lower than average rate, other employers would have to be taxed at rates above the average.

Although Table 1 shows only state taxes, each employer would have to pay a federal tax in addition. Currently the federal tax amounts to 0.7 percent of taxable wages (see note 3), which is about 0.35 percent of total wages. An average employer's total unemployment insurance tax rate would be the sum of the percentage in Table 1 plus 0.35 percent. In Rhode Island, for example, this total tax rate would be 4.15 percent.

The distribution of the state and federal unemployment taxes paid by employers is shown in Figure 1.[6] The top four boxes at the right of the chart

5

Figure 1
Federal-State Unemployment Insurance System:
Sources of Funds in Fiscal 1976

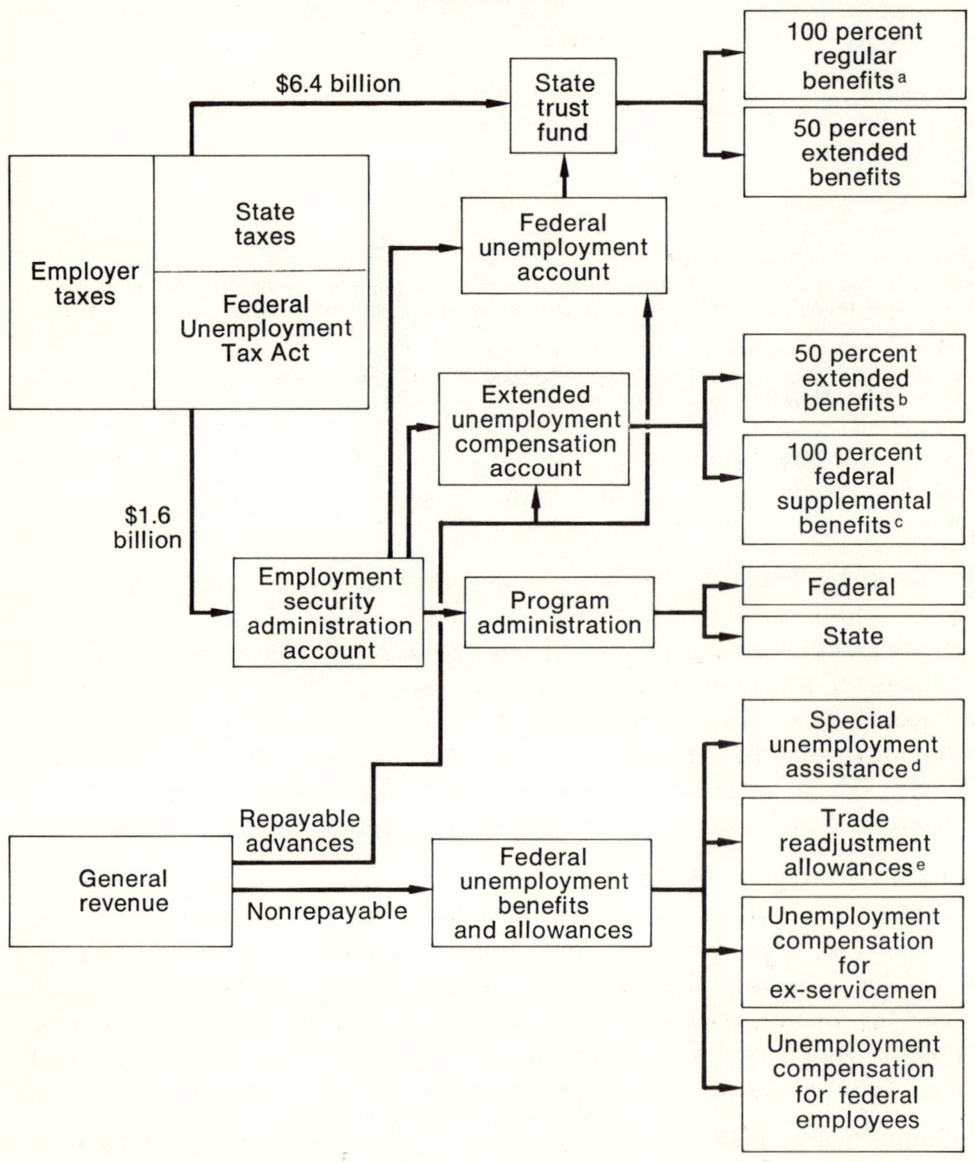

a Under state unemployment insurance laws.
b Under the Federal-State Extended Unemployment Compensation Act of 1970, sections 201–207 of P.L. 91-373.
c Under the Emergency Unemployment Compensation Act of 1974, P.L. 93-572.
d Under the Emergency Jobs and Unemployment Assistance Act of 1974, P.L. 93-567.
e Under the Trade Act of 1974, sections 221–224 of P.L. 93-618.

Note: Sources of funds include employee contributions for the states of Alabama, Alaska, and New Jersey.

Source: U.S. Department of Labor, Employment and Training Administration, Unemployment Insurance Service, September 1977.

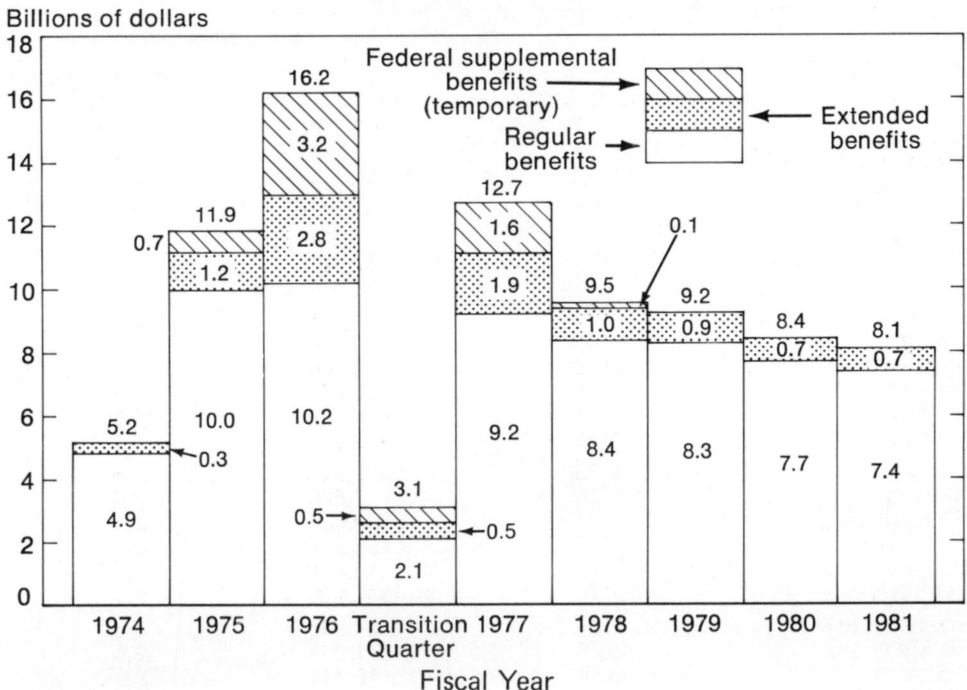

Note: 1974 through transition quarter actual; 1977–1981 estimated.
Source: U.S. Department of Labor, Employment and Training Administration, Unemployment Insurance Service, September 1977.

show three kinds of benefits which are paid under the unemployment insurance system: regular benefits, which are financed entirely by the state tax; extended benefits, which are paid under a permanent standby program that goes into operation when unemployment is unusually high and which are financed jointly by state and federal taxes on the employer; and federal supplemental benefits, which are temporary emergency benefits legislated by Congress during the recent recession and which are financed entirely by a federal tax on employers. The relative costs of these various benefits in recent years are shown in Figure 2.

Throughout most of the life of the unemployment insurance program, which began in 1935, the federal tax has been used to cover only costs of administration (the fifth and sixth boxes on the right-hand side of Figure 1). In recent years, however, it has been used for some benefit payments, namely, half the benefits in the extended benefit program and all the benefits in the federal supplemental benefits program.

Table 2
Outstanding Loans to States from Federal Unemployment Account,
August 15, 1977

State	Date of First Loan	Amount of Loans Outstanding Thousands of dollars	As percentage of total 1976 payroll
Alabama	12/75	56,660	0.6
Arkansas	1/76	30,000	0.6
Connecticut	3/72	438,130	3.3
Delaware	11/75	36,600	1.5
District of Columbia	11/75	52,400	1.2
Hawaii	1/76	22,500	0.7
Illinois	12/75	751,600	2.0
Maine	9/75	22,900	0.9
Maryland	3/76	62,659	0.6
Massachusetts	4/75	265,000	1.3
Michigan	4/75	624,000	1.7
Minnesota	7/75	172,000	1.2
Montana	4/76	9,284	0.5
Nevada	1/76	7,600	0.3
New Jersey	1/75	638,902	2.5
New York	2/77	155,750	0.2
Oregon	2/76	18,450	0.2
Pennsylvania	10/75	847,296	2.1
Puerto Rico	4/75	67,000	2.2
Rhode Island	2/75	71,074	2.4
Vermont	2/74	46,444	3.9
Washington	4/73	137,218	1.2
Total		4,533,467	0.6

Source: U.S. Department of Labor, Employment and Training Administration, Unemployment Insurance Service, September 1977.

The balances in the unemployment insurance trust funds of some nineteen states, as shown in Table 1, are negative. These states had to borrow from the federal unemployment insurance account and are currently under obligation to repay the loans. Table 2 shows the amount of state debts to the federal account as of August 15, 1977. (Since that date, Oregon has repaid its debt, but other states have increased theirs. As of March 1978, the aggregate of state debts had grown to over $5 billion.) The last column of Table 2 shows each state's debt as a percentage of that state's total 1976 payroll. If a state wished to pay off its entire debt in one year, this percentage is the *additional* average tax it would have to impose on all its employers during that year.

The debts shown in Table 2 represent payments of regular benefits and each state's share of extended benefits. In addition to these debts owed by the individual states, there is another debt owed collectively by all U.S. employers. The federal extended unemployment compensation account was used to pay the federal share of extended benefits and all federal supplemental benefits.

8

When this federal account ran out of funds, it borrowed from general revenues. As of August 1977, the debt owed by all employers collectively to the extended unemployment compensation account amounted to $8.7 billion dollars. Of this total, $2.9 billion represented the federal share of extended benefits, and $5.8 billion represented federal supplemental benefit payments. Thus, as of August 1977, the nation's employers owed through their states a total debt of $13.2 billion. The total debt consisted of the $4.5 billion owed by the twenty-one states individually to the federal unemployment account plus the $8.7 billion owed by all states collectively to the extended unemployment compensation account.

In addition to paying off these debts, employers must supply not only the funds needed for current benefits but also funds to restore reserves to an adequate level. This triple burden is reflected in the average tax rates shown in Table 1—to which must be added, as mentioned earlier, 0.35 percent of total wages to be paid to the federal government. Under present law, funds for all benefits—regular benefits, state and federal shares of extended benefits, and past federal payments of federal supplemental benefits—must come from the same source, namely, a tax on covered employers.

Causes of the Dilemma

The current financial dilemma is traceable to three principal causes. The first and most important cause was simply an unusual amount of unemployment in calendar years 1975 and 1976. The national unemployment rate for insured workers was 6.8 in 1975 and 4.6 in 1976. The national average benefit-cost rate (benefits as a percentage of total wages) was 2.03 percent in 1975 and 1.39 in 1976. By contrast, in 1969 the unemployment rate for insured workers was only 2.1 percent, and the benefit-cost rate was only 0.58 percent. (The benefits used in the calculation of these benefit-cost rates are regular benefits only.) While the 1975 rate was not unique (in 1958 the unemployment rate for insured workers was 6.6 percent and the benefit-cost rate was 2.05 percent), it was unusual for two consecutive years to have such high rates. The state funds had no adequate opportunity to recover from the first blow before the second one was upon them. In addition, the system had to bear the cost of the extended benefits and the federal supplemental benefits programs.

The second cause of the financial dilemma was congressional action that extended the duration of benefits during recessions. In addition to the extended benefit program, which paid benefits for up to thirty-nine weeks and was made permanent in 1970, Congress provided for payment of benefits over an even longer period by a series of emergency enactments during the recent recession. Payment of benefits was extended for up to fifty-two weeks in

December 1974, and for up to sixty-five weeks in March 1975. As noted above, these congressionally mandated programs of extended duration eventually resulted in a debt of $8.7 billion which, under existing law, must be recovered by the imposition of a higher tax on covered employers. The relative sizes of the three benefit programs in the recent years may be seen in Figure 2. (Note that Figure 2 shows fiscal years.)

A third possible cause of the current financial dilemma in the case of some states was failure to build up an adequate reserve before the recession struck. This was true of about a dozen states at most and is a less important cause of difficulty for the program as a whole than are the other two.

OPTIONS FOR RESOLVING THE DILEMMA

There are three principal ways to meet the current financing dilemma. The first option is to do nothing, that is, to allow existing law to govern the allocation of costs. Under this option, there would be the least amount of sharing of the program's financial burdens. Each state would continue to be responsible for building up its own reserve fund, including the repayment of its debt to the federal unemployment account. The states would have to impose average tax rates of 0.35 percent of total wages plus the percentages shown in Table 1. In addition, the federal government would need to impose an increased uniform tax on all covered employers in order to recover the advances made from general revenues to the extended unemployment compensation account. At the present federal tax rate of 0.7 percent on taxable wages of $6,000, the collective debt of all the states to the extended unemployment compensation account would be repaid by about 1986. If Congress were to waive the federal supplemental benefits debts, as many groups including the Federal Advisory Council on unemployment insurance have urged, the extended unemployment compensation account debt would be repaid by about 1982. If the first option is chosen the entire burden will be borne by the payroll tax rather than being paid in part from general revenues. Furthermore, each state would continue to bear its own costs, and hard-pressed states would not be able to shift some of their burden onto other states.

A second option is to spread the burden of the employers' tax uniformly among the states. This can be done by taxing all covered employers in the country, putting the receipts into a central fund, and paying subsidies to states according to the severity of their unemployment.

The third option resembles the second except for its source of funds. Instead of raising the money by a uniform tax on all covered employers, general revenues would be used, and all taxpayers would share the burden. This option presents the greatest degree of burden sharing and is the one chosen by the drafters of the two bills analyzed below.

The sharing concept included in the last two options could be applied both to past and future benefits, or it could apply only to the future or only to the past. If applied only to the past, it would be used to lift the unemployment insurance system out of its present financial hole but not to change the system permanently. This approach is not reflected in either bill, but it may be advanced in the course of legislative consideration.

CONTENT AND ORIGINS OF NEW FINANCING PROPOSALS

Summary of Bills

The financing provisions of the bills introduced by Representative Brodhead (H.R. 8292) and Senator Javits (S. 1853) are compared in Table 3. Both bills would provide for use of federal general tax revenues to assist those states that are experiencing unusually heavy unemployment. Both bills would apply retroactively, the Brodhead bill to 1974 and the Javits bill to 1975. Both bills require, as a condition of eligibility, that a state's unemployment rate for insured workers be at least 6 percent, and that the benefit payments in the year for which reimbursement is sought exceed the payments required by experience in a base year. The benefit payments for which reimbursement could be obtained would not include any payments for which a state is already being reimbursed under state or federal law. Excluded, therefore, are reimbursements for state payments of federal supplemental benefits, the federal share of extended benefits, payments of unemployment compensation to federal employees and certain ex-service personnel.

The two bills define base-year experience somewhat differently, but both provide for a federal subsidy of a portion of the difference between current-year experience and base-year experience. Both bills would increase the rate of subsidy as the rate of unemployment increases. Although the Javits bill provides a more generous subsidy than does the Brodhead bill, at no point is a state relieved of all responsibility for its own unemployment costs. A significant difference between the two bills is in the way they compute the insured unemployment rate. The Javits bill adds to the number of the unemployed all claimants for supplemental benefits and one-fourth of those who have exhausted their benefits. As a result, the 6 percent unemployment rate for insured employees in the Javits bill approximates a total unemployment rate of 6 percent, while the 6 percent unemployment rate for insured employees in the Brodhead bill approximates a total unemployment rate of 8 percent. The Brodhead bill thus reflects a "catastrophe" approach to a greater extent than does the Javits bill.

The cost of the Brodhead bill for three years, 1974–1976, has been estimated at $4.1 billion, while that of the Javits bill for 1975 and 1976 has been estimated at a much higher cost of $6.8 billion. The principal reasons for the higher cost of the Javits proposal are the more generous reimbursement rates and the broader definition of insured unemployment rate.

Table 3

**Comparison of Cost Equalization Provisions
of H.R. 8292 and S. 1853**

Provision	H.R. 8292	S. 1853
Retroactive effective date	1974	1975
Eligible state	Unemployment rate for insured workers (IUR) at least 6 percent and benefit payments in excess of payments in base year	IUR at least 6 percent and benefit payments in excess of annual base amount
Definition of base year or base amount	Base year is most recent year in past five for which state's IUR was less than 6 percent (if IUR not less than 6 percent in any of past five years, base year is year in past five in which amount of payments was least)	Annual base amount is average annual benefit cost of lowest three years in past five (if IUR not less than 6 percent in any of past five years, base amount is amount in year in past five in which amount of payments was least)
Federal grant	The share of excess benefit costs (amount by which state benefit payments for one year exceed the base year or the annual base amount)	

	State IUR (percent)	Percent of excess state benefit costs	State IUR (percent)	Percent of excess state benefit costs
	6.0 but less than 6.5	25	6.0 but less than 7.0	50
	6.5 but less than 7.0	37.5	7.0 but less than 8.0	66.67
	7.0 or more	50	8.0 or more	75

Provision	H.R. 8292	S. 1853
Financing	General revenues	General revenues
Cost	1974–1976 (3 years) $4,179 million	1975–1976 (2 years) $6,870 million
Computation of IUR	Average weekly number of claims for regular, extended, and additional benefits divided by average monthly employment in four consecutive calendar quarters ending June 30	Average weekly number of claims for regular, additionally extended, and supplemental benefits, and one fourth of individuals who have received final payment during the specified thirteen-week period, divided by average monthly employment for the first four of most recent six calendar quarters

14

Both bills combine two elements—reinsurance and cost equalization—which for the sake of clarity should be recognized as distinct, at least in principle. The rationale for reinsurance is uncertainty; the rationale for cost equalization is inequity. The answer to "Why have a reinsurance scheme?" is that no state is safe from a sudden, unforeseen rise in its unemployment benefit-cost rate. The answer to "Why have a cost equalization scheme?" is that a state may be burdened with a benefit-cost rate that is "too high," whether or not the rate is foreseen. Often, the terms reinsurance and cost equalization are mistakenly used interchangeably.

Reinsurance

Some form of reinsurance is a customary part of most large insurance plans. It is simply an additional application of the insurance technique, which substitutes a small certain loss (the premium or tax) for a large uncertain loss (a sudden leap in costs). Reinsurance is a form of insurance against catastrophe. Each member of a group of insurers contributes to a central fund to support any member who has an extraordinarily unfavorable experience. Reinsurance relieves all the insurers of the necessity of accumulating excessively large reserves to meet the occasional catastrophic event.

In the case of unemployment insurance, the technique of reinsurance has the same objective as cost equalization insofar as both are intended to ease the lot of states that experience unusual unemployment. But reinsurance differs in that the norm of "excessive" unemployment is a state's own experience, not that of other states. If a state's benefit-cost rate in a given year exceeds its "normal" rate, the state becomes eligible for a grant from a central fund. The state's "normal" rate may be calculated in various ways (for example, by taking an average of recent years or by taking the lowest year in a recent period), and the amount of excess required to trigger a grant may be large or small. The grant may make up a part or the whole of the excess costs.

In a pure case of reinsurance it is not possible to predict which states are likely to receive a grant. In this respect, reinsurance fulfills an essential condition of any genuine insurance, namely, that the actual occurrence insured against be uncertain. Reinsurance does not permit a state to remain eligible for a grant indefinitely.

Reinsurance is intended as protection against rates of unemployment that are occasional and unforeseen, not as protection against either seasonal or chronic unemployment. Typically, reinsurance is the proper safeguard against natural disasters, wars, political disturbances such as an oil embargo, or the initial impact of the shutdown of a major industry. Reinsurance is generally considered as protection against cyclical unemployment. To the extent that some states are predictably more cyclically sensitive than others, however, any reinsurance program will contain an element of cost equalization.

In a pure form of reinsurance the subsidy is provided by the collective insurers. To the extent that the subsidy comes from a source outside the insurance system itself, the arrangement resembles a form of cost equalization, with the sharing occurring not among the insurers but between the insurers and an outside body. Such reinsurance should probably be thought of as a hybrid form and, for clarity's sake, should not be described as reinsurance.

Proposals in the unemployment insurance field for some form of reinsurance have a long history, having been considered by the Committee on Economic Security in 1934 and by the Social Security Board in the early 1940s. New proposals continue to be offered periodically. Although bearing the title of "reinsurance," the proposals often are in fact cost equalization plans, as was, for example, the 1950 bill of the Truman administration, H.R. 8059, 81st Congress. The Federal Advisory Council turned its attention to a form of reinsurance in 1952 but was unable to agree on anything more than a document setting forth the relative advantages of loans and "reinsurance grants."

A genuine reinsurance plan was put forward in 1953 by Milton O. Loysen, administrator of the New York employment security agency. Loysen's background was, appropriately enough, in insurance. In 1963 the Benefit Financing Committee of the Interstate Conference of Employment Security Agencies (ICESA) produced a refined version of the Loysen plan. Under the ICESA plan, called catastrophe reinsurance, funds would be provided by a tax on all states, and a state would become eligible for a grant when its benefit-cost rate exceeded 1.6 times its own average rate over the preceding five years. The grant would cover 60 percent of this excess cost.

Cost Equalization

Cost equalization, like reinsurance, provides a subsidy for states that have experienced unusually high costs for unemployment insurance. The principal difference is the way in which "unusual" is defined. In cost equalization, the norm is not a state's own previous experience but some absolute norm that applies to all states at all times. The states that have a benefit-cost rate higher than this norm are reimbursed from a central fund for all or for a portion of the excess costs. The norms most frequently proposed have been either the average benefit-cost rate of all states or a benefit-cost rate of 2 percent of total wages. (The benefit-cost rate is the ratio of benefits to wages, usually total wages, over a certain period, usually a year.) The rationale for cost equalization is not uncertainty but inability. A state is assumed to be unable to meet a benefit-cost rate above 2 percent of total wages. Just as the reason for reinsurance is the unforeseen nature of the burden, the reason for cost equalization is the excessive size of the burden, even though it is foreseen.

In a cost equalization program, as distinguished from a reinsurance program, it is possible to predict which states are more likely to receive equalization grants, and there is nothing to prevent a state from receiving a grant every year. If the revenues are derived from the federal unemployment tax, it is possible to measure the probable extent to which some states will subsidize other states.

Proposals for cost equalization have a long history. First discussed by the Committee on Economic Security in 1934, proposals for cost equalization have surfaced repeatedly over the years—for example, in 1944 (S. 1730), in 1950 (H.R. 8059), in 1952 (H.R. 6954), in 1959 (H.R. 3547), and in 1965 (H.R. 8282).

Reinsurance and Cost Equalization Combined

H.R. 8292 and S. 1853 combine the concepts of reinsurance and cost equalization ingeniously. The primary objective of the bills is reinsurance, that is, to provide against the occasional unforeseen excessive benefit-cost rate. Overlaying this basic characteristic of reinsurance are several features of cost equalization. One is the requirement that a state's unemployment rate for insured workers be at least 6 percent (equivalent to an 8 percent total unemployment rate and to a 2 percent total benefit-cost rate). Here the norm is not relative to the state's own experience but is an absolute measure of "excessive" unemployment.

Under this norm, some states will be more likely to profit from the program than others. States that regularly have higher than average levels of unemployment (seasonal, cyclical, or chronic), such as Washington, Michigan, or Massachusetts, will be eligible for a subsidy more often than states with lower than average unemployment, such as Texas, Ohio, or Virginia. Figure 3 provides a rough measure of the probability that some states will receive a larger and more frequent subsidy than others. The chart is based on benefit-cost rates rather than unemployment rates; but, since unemployment is the chief determinant of cost (it outweighs all other factors combined), these long-term average cost rates may be taken as a proxy for unemployment rates and hence as a measure of the probability that a given state will benefit from the proposed program. It is in this probability—predictability—that the element of cost equalization appears.

According to those most active in constructing the original plan, the provision requiring a 6 percent unemployment rate for insured workers was inserted not primarily with a view to cost equalization but merely to perform the same kind of function as that of the "deductible" clause in automobile insurance policies. Without such a provision, states could be eligible for reinsurance grants even though their level of unemployment was very low.

Figure 3
Average Benefit-Cost Rate under State Unemployment Compensation Laws, 1940–1975

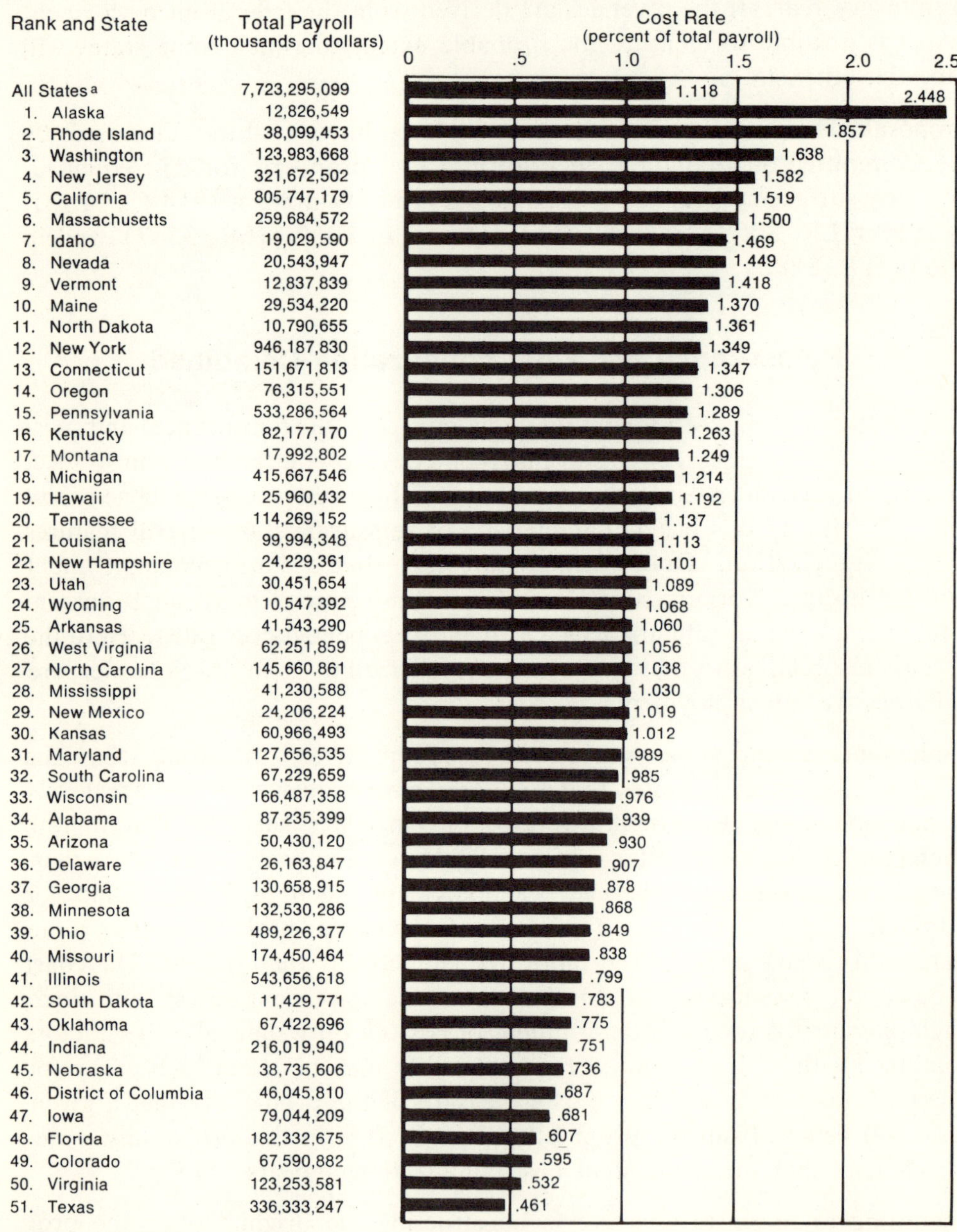

Rank and State	Total Payroll (thousands of dollars)	Cost Rate (percent of total payroll)
All States[a]	7,723,295,099	1.118
1. Alaska	12,826,549	2.448
2. Rhode Island	38,099,453	1.857
3. Washington	123,983,668	1.638
4. New Jersey	321,672,502	1.582
5. California	805,747,179	1.519
6. Massachusetts	259,684,572	1.500
7. Idaho	19,029,590	1.469
8. Nevada	20,543,947	1.449
9. Vermont	12,837,839	1.418
10. Maine	29,534,220	1.370
11. North Dakota	10,790,655	1.361
12. New York	946,187,830	1.349
13. Connecticut	151,671,813	1.347
14. Oregon	76,315,551	1.306
15. Pennsylvania	533,286,564	1.289
16. Kentucky	82,177,170	1.263
17. Montana	17,992,802	1.249
18. Michigan	415,667,546	1.214
19. Hawaii	25,960,432	1.192
20. Tennessee	114,269,152	1.137
21. Louisiana	99,994,348	1.113
22. New Hampshire	24,229,361	1.101
23. Utah	30,451,654	1.089
24. Wyoming	10,547,392	1.068
25. Arkansas	41,543,290	1.060
26. West Virginia	62,251,859	1.056
27. North Carolina	145,660,861	1.038
28. Mississippi	41,230,588	1.030
29. New Mexico	24,206,224	1.019
30. Kansas	60,966,493	1.012
31. Maryland	127,656,535	.989
32. South Carolina	67,229,659	.985
33. Wisconsin	166,487,358	.976
34. Alabama	87,235,399	.939
35. Arizona	50,430,120	.930
36. Delaware	26,163,847	.907
37. Georgia	130,658,915	.878
38. Minnesota	132,530,286	.868
39. Ohio	489,226,377	.849
40. Missouri	174,450,464	.838
41. Illinois	543,656,618	.799
42. South Dakota	11,429,771	.783
43. Oklahoma	67,422,696	.775
44. Indiana	216,019,940	.751
45. Nebraska	38,735,606	.736
46. District of Columbia	46,045,810	.687
47. Iowa	79,044,209	.681
48. Florida	182,332,675	.607
49. Colorado	67,590,882	.595
50. Virginia	123,253,581	.532
51. Texas	336,333,247	.461

[a] Excludes data for Puerto Rico.

Note: Cumulative total of benefits paid plus benefit reserves as percent of cumulative total covered payroll. Data from U.S. Department of Labor, based on tabulations by state agencies, may not add because of rounding.

Source: Division of Research and Statistics, Ohio Bureau of Employment Services, Columbus, no. A-524, 1977.

Since this program was considered to be catastrophe insurance, some floor had to be provided—in this case a floor of 6 percent unemployment rate for insured employees (roughly equivalent to a total unemployment rate of 8 percent in the Brodhead bill and 6 percent in the Javits bill).

The use of general revenues is the second element of cost equalization. The introduction of funds from outside the insurance system definitely differentiates the proposed program from insurance as that term is normally used. Payments under the program are more properly termed grants or subsidies than reinsurance payments.

The program would become measurable more like reinsurance if the source of revenues were a tax on covered employers, as it was in the original version of this proposal. If, in addition, the tax were experience-rated, so that states which frequently drew from the fund would eventually pay a somewhat higher rate, the program would become reinsurance in a complete sense.

Role of ICESA

The basic structure of the present bills is traceable to work begun by the Interstate Conference of Employment Security Agencies over a decade ago. In the aftermath of the 1958 recession and its legacy of financial problems, the Benefit Financing Committee of ICESA began a study of the situation. By 1961 the committee had a reinsurance plan, which it revised in 1962 and 1963. At the same time, the Kennedy and Johnson administrations were proposing cost equalization plans (in 1961, 1963, and 1965). The final 1963 plan of ICESA was almost identical to the Brodhead bill, except that the source of its funds was a tax on covered employers and the program would not apply retroactively.

In 1963, the states were polled on this reinsurance plan, but only four replies were received, all negative. At its 1963 meeting in Omaha, Nebraska, ICESA voted not to take a position on the issue. Polled again in 1964, the states responded in greater numbers but still negatively, with only four favorable votes. (The alternative cost equalization plan prepared by ICESA received only two favorable votes.) A "reinsurance" plan financed by federal revenues was included in the Johnson administration bill, H.R. 8282, in 1966, but was opposed by ICESA at its meeting in Phoenix, Arizona, that year. The plan died when Congress failed to enact H.R. 8282.

In 1974, when a recession had again focused attention on state financial problems, a special ICESA task force was appointed to develop proposals for financial aid to the states. The task force returned to the 1963 plan but added a provision for retroactive application. At this stage, the source of funds was still to be a 0.1 percent federal tax on covered payrolls. In a poll of the states in late 1975 the plan was approved as the official ICESA position. The vote was thirty states in favor of the plan and nineteen states against it. The affirmative vote represented 63.5 percent of the average amount of employment and 65.3 percent of all employers in the system.

The nineteen states voting against the proposal were: Colorado, District of Columbia, Georgia, Indiana, Minnesota, Mississippi, Missouri, Nebraska, Nevada, New Hampshire, New Mexico, North Carolina, Ohio, Oklahoma, South Carolina, South Dakota, Texas, Utah, and Virginia. As shown in Figure 3, these states have experienced less than average benefit costs, except for Nevada, which still voted against the proposal. Eleven states with below average benefit costs voted in favor of the ICESA proposal: Alabama, Arizona, Arkansas, Delaware, Illinois, Iowa, Kansas, Maryland, West Virginia, Wisconsin, and Wyoming. Of these, all but Iowa, Kansas, and Wyoming would receive a subsidy from the retroactive provisions of the proposal (see Table 3). In 1977 the ICESA proposal was altered to make use of general revenues instead of the payroll tax, and again the states were polled. The use of federal revenues was approved by member organizations in thirty-nine states with 73 percent of the covered employment.

What explains the shift in the states' position on reinsurance? There seem to be three reasons. The first is undoubtedly the unprecedented scope of the current financing dilemma. Whereas the 1958 recession had forced three states to borrow, the 1975–1976 recession placed almost half the states in that humbling position. The second is the retroactive provision, which will not only provide help for some indefinite future situation but also bring immediate substantial aid to a majority (thirty-seven) of the states, especially those whose reserves were most depleted by the recent recession (see Tables 3 and 1). The third reason is the shift from the payroll tax to general revenues, with a consequent broadening of the tax base and an obscuring of the tax incidence. Each state can see what it will receive; what it will pay is less clear.

INSURANCE VERSUS ASSISTANCE

Financing is crucial to unemployment insurance not only to provide the necessary funds but also to establish its insurance character. The essential difference between social insurance and social assistance (welfare) is that social insurance benefits are considered to be an earned right. In the eyes of society, that right rests on the method of financing the program. Because unemployment insurance draws its funds from an earmarked tax on the act of working, it is possible to consider unemployment benefits as deferred wages, in the sense that wages would probably be higher if employers did not have to pay the payroll tax. In any case, the payroll tax makes unemployment benefits a regular cost of doing business, like wages and other economic costs. It is this integration with the market system that gives unemployment benefits their characteristic of an earned right.

In the United States, this market relation is emphasized by two additional characteristics: within the total system, each state is responsible for its own costs, and within each state the individual employer usually pays an experience-rated tax, that is, a tax that is proportional to his own experience with unemployment. Both characteristics have been the center of much controversy over the life of the program, but thus far they have been retained.

Any modification that weakens the market relation of the unemployment insurance program also weakens the basis for identifying it as social insurance rather than social assistance. Some modifications of the market relation already exist—for example, the ceiling on the maximum tax rate that may be imposed on any employer, no matter how great his cost to the common fund. Such modifications reflect the significance of the adjective in the term, "*social* insurance."

Thus, unemployment insurance as social insurance is a hybrid, standing somewhere between wages paid because of market performance and welfare benefits paid because of individual need. It partakes of both. The bills under discussion move the unemployment insurance program somewhat away from the market and toward welfare. This effect is clear and is not under debate. What is under debate are the relative gains and losses produced by the shift.

The principal arguments for and against the bills are based either on economic considerations or on what, for want of a better term, may be called intrinsic considerations. That is, they are based on the effects of the bills on the unemployment insurance program or on the economy. The economic arguments in turn involve the effects of the bills on either the state economies or on the national economy as a whole.

IMPACT ON THE UNEMPLOYMENT INSURANCE PROGRAM

Arguments for the Bills

Avoid Failure of Present Program. The changes proposed in the pending bills would lessen the risk of the financial collapse of the existing program. Providing assistance for previous years would enable hard-pressed states to climb out of the financial hole that the recent recession left them in. Assistance in future years would help prevent the recurrence of past difficulties. Although benefits would continue to be paid without the proposed changes (as they were during the last recession), it is argued that a collapse of state financing would probably bring about a restructuring of the present system, with the federal government taking over the program and its control. The concern is not so much that the few states with very high unemployment *could* not maintain their fiscal solvency but that they *would* not. They would be tempted to take the easy way out, that is, to maintain benefits, neglect to raise taxes, and eventually let the federal government shoulder the entire burden.

Smaller State Reserves Would Be Required. The proposed changes essentially provide reinsurance. Adequate levels of protection could be maintained with smaller state reserves because reinsurances would protect the states from the cost of unusually high levels of unemployment. Some form of reinsurance is a normal part of every large insurance system faced with a possible catastrophe.

Strengthen Present Program. Lightening the burden borne by states with heavy unemployment would make it easier for these states to maintain adequate benefit levels and reasonable disqualification provisions. The states with the most unemployment are the large industrial states. Since most of the covered workers live in these states, it is important for the general health of the unemployment insurance system that these states maintain an effective program.

New York, for example, has been a leader in liberalizing unemployment insurance. Because its economy has been trailing the national average in recent years, the New York legislature has become cautious about increasing benefits. In states with above average unemployment and above average taxes employers frequently cite high taxes in contending that benefits should not be increased and disqualification provisions should be tightened.

The availability of general revenues to cover part of the extra costs of unemployment insurance at unusual levels of unemployment would enable states to extend the duration of benefits. In the last recession, the availability of general revenues permitted the extension of benefit payments up to sixty-five weeks.

Proponents claim there is little likelihood that the proposed subsidies would encourage states to abuse the system, that is, to liberalize their programs irresponsibly. At least two safeguards are provided against such abuse. First, the subsidy is triggered not by the cost of benefits, over which the state has direct control, but by its unemployment rate, over which the state has little control. Second, the subsidy would never cover the entire excess cost. A state which liberalizes its program—in amount or duration of benefits or conditions of eligibility—must always expect to bear part of the burden itself, no matter how high the cost.

Opposing Arguments

Present Program Will Not Fail. Opponents deny that the unemployment program faces a financial crisis that will force changes. They point out that the tax rates shown in Table 1 are based on the assumption of a five-year period in which to recover from the past recession, and that only a half dozen states are faced with an average tax rate as high as 3 percent (on total payrolls). If the period were lengthened the tax rate would be lower. This 3 percent tax rate is low compared with other labor costs—or even compared with fringe benefits or the social security tax. Since the unemployment insurance tax, unlike other costs, will not continue at a high level indefinitely, opponents believe that the employers in these few states can afford to pay the tax.

Reinsurance Is Not Required. Opponents contend that a loan program would meet the needs of the unemployment insurance system just as well as reinsurance would. A loan program, which has been a part of the system for most of its life, has permitted the individual states to keep lower reserves than would otherwise be required. The only difference between a loan program and reinsurance is that loans must be repaid. Opponents contend, as noted in the previous argument, that states can meet their own costs and repay their loans.

Benefit Levels Can Be Improved without the Proposed Change. Opponents contend that the liberality of a state's unemployment insurance program is less a function of cost than of the state's general political climate and the political strength of organized labor. They deny that there is any close (negative) correlation between a state's average unemployment and the adequacy of its unemployment insurance program. The large industrialized states that have the most unemployment seem to have the most adequate unemployment insurance programs.[7]

Moreover, opponents point to the possibility of abuse of the unemployment insurance program. William Papier, longtime director of research in the Ohio unemployment insurance system, has described the many ways a state can manipulate its unemployment rate for insured employees through both its definition and its measurement of unemployment.

Opponents contend that the problems that are facing the welfare and social security programs in Congress may be duplicated in the unemployment insurance program if it becomes dependent on general revenues. Indeed, Congress has recently legislated to tighten up some specific disqualification provisions in the unemployment insurance program because some congressmen feared that the program was getting out of hand.

Opponents reject the claim that the pending legislation poses no threat to the element of social insurance in the program. An essential distinction between social insurance and social assistance (welfare) is that insurance benefits are claimed as an earned right, primarily because benefits are directly related to the previous work and earnings of the beneficiary. In the United States, where each state is responsible for its own unemployment insurance costs, and where each employer is taxed in some proportion to the firm's own unemployment experience, a solid case can be made that unemployment benefits are largely deferred wages. The proposed bills are a step away from this direct relation between the employee's work and his entitlement to benefits.

Opponents are primarily concerned that taking this step could lead to other changes that would weaken the insurance characteristic of the program and increase its welfare characteristic. "Excessive" unemployment is defined in the bills as an insured unemployment rate of 6 percent, but no evidence is offered to show that this rate is in fact excessive. If changes are to be based on such loose impressions of excessive unemployment, opponents charge, what is to prevent Congress from lowering that figure in order to add a greater measure of welfare to the program. Proposals might also be made to subsidize a greater proportion of that excessive cost. Opponents argue that there is a constant attempt on the part of all economic agents to escape the discipline of the market. Once cost equalization is accepted without strong proof that it is needed, the insurance principle has been abandoned and there remains no reliable constraint against successive steps in the direction of pure welfare. The evolution of S. 1853 demonstrates just such a progressive liberalization—from the original ICESA proposal to the later ICESA proposal to the current Javits bill. Many agree that the introduction of more federal funds—whether general revenues or a federal unemployment insurance tax, but especially the former—will bring more federal control over the unemployment insurance system.

IMPACT ON STATE ECONOMIES

Pattern of Subsidies to States

Table 4, column 1, provides an estimate of the subsidies that would be paid to each state under H.R. 8292 for the three-year period 1974–1976. (Under S. 1853 the subsidies would be larger, but the relative shares of the states would be roughly the same.) Clearly some states would receive much larger subsidies than others. Since the states are economic entities in competition with one another, this differential impact becomes an important political consideration for the states' representatives in Congress.

Ten states, accounting for 46.6 percent of covered employment, would receive 79 percent of the subsidies.[8] Of the ten, eight are in the northern part of the country, five in the Northeast. Not unexpectedly, the snow belt would receive more than the sun belt, a pattern that would probably recur. States that receive the subsidies would have financed them in part by taxes paid into general revenues. The more industrialized, richer states of the North probably would have made a greater contribution to their own subsidies than certain other states. The general pattern of federal taxes and subsidies probably still reflects an earlier situation in which government programs provided a net flow from the richer North to the poorer South.

The original ICESA proposal would have financed unemployment insurance subsidies by a uniform 0.1 percent increase in the federal tax on covered employers. Column 2 of Table 4 shows the estimated amounts that each state would have contributed under such an arrangement, and column 3 shows the net subsidy, that is, the amount by which the additional payments to states would exceed the taxes paid by each state. The net subsidies are less than the gross subsidies, but the amounts are still substantial and the same states remain the principal beneficiaries. Seventeen states are shown as sustaining net losses, that is, they would pay in more than they would take out. In most cases these losses would grow larger over time. Some states, such as South Carolina and Illinois, would clearly gain from retroactive application of the proposal, but they probably would not gain from its future application because of their generally low average level of unemployment (see Figure 3).

States that expect to gain from the proposed program are likely to favor its enactment. States that do not expect to gain from it are likely to oppose it. There are, however, other general considerations which deserve examination.

Table 4

**Subsidies, Gross and Net, Receivable by States
under H.R. 8292, 1974–1976**

(thousands of dollars)

	Gross Subsidy (1)	Reinsurance Tax[a] (2)	Net Subsidy (1) minus (2) (3)
Alabama	53,022	11,883.0	41,139.0
Alaska	36,227	4,069.1	32,157.9
Arizona	39,952	7,611.9	32,340.1
Arkansas	32,816	6,357.0	26,459.0
California	466,523	93,719.7	372,803.3
Colorado	0	9,372.1	−9,372.1
Connecticut	145,157	15,199.7	129,957.3
Delaware	6,893	2,349.1	4,543.9
District of Columbia	0	3,947.3	−3,947.3
Florida	60,043	29,882.7	30,160.3
Georgia	43,604	19,771.5	23,832.5
Hawaii	3,422	4,615.3	−1,193.3
Idaho	2,785	2,990.3	−205.3
Illinois	316,706	46,178.2	270,527.8
Indiana	43,264	20,439.9	22,824.1
Iowa	0	10,066.5	−10,066.5
Kansas	0	7,508.4	−7,508.4
Kentucky	33,448	10,331.2	23,116.8
Louisiana	0	12,641.7	−12,641.7
Maine	22,648	3,449.8	19,198.2
Maryland	29,738	13,790.8	15,947.2
Massachusetts	192,583	22,076.6	170,506.4
Michigan	706,619	35,285.9	671,333.1
Minnesota	0	16,232.9	−16,232.9
Mississippi	11,387	6,944.7	4,442.3
Missouri	57,250	17,328.9	39,921.1
Montana	4,092	2,313.8	1,778.2
Nebraska	0	4,846.7	−4,846.7
Nevada	12,187	3,631.5	8,555.5
New Hampshire	10,751	3,006.9	7,744.1
New Jersey	323,873	31,269.5	292,603.5
New Mexico	2,522	3,243.6	−721.6
New York	414,152	68,802.2	345,349.8
North Carolina	132,095	21,079.3	111,015.7
North Dakota	0	1,595.2	−1,595.2
Ohio	0	41,489.5	−41,489.5
Oklahoma	0	8,651.3	−8,651.3
Oregon	42,162	10,280.6	31,881.4
Pennsylvania	428,215	44,422.0	383,793.0
Puerto Rico	94,587	8,080.3	86,506.7
Rhode Island	49,363	3,719.8	45,643.2
South Carolina	66,026	9,989.6	56,036.4
South Dakota	0	1,612.7	−1,612.7
Tennessee	54,156	15,054.0	39,102.0
Texas	0	47,245.6	−47,245.6
Utah	0	4,125.7	−4,125.7
Vermont	8,913	1,560.0	7,353.0
Virginia	0	16,949.4	−16,949.4

28

Table 4 (continued)

	Gross Subsidy (1)	Reinsurance Tax[a] (2)	Net Subsidy (1) minus (2) (3)
Washington	130,766	16,747.8	114,018.2
West Virginia	8,861	5,973.7	2,887.3
Wisconsin	81,965	19,357.4	62,607.6
Wyoming	0	1,473.4	− 1,473.4

[a] Assuming subsidies are financed by 0.1 percent federal tax on covered payrolls.
Source: U.S. Department of Labor, Employment and Training Administration, Unemployment Insurance Service, September 1977.

Proposals to solve the current financing dilemma by a system of subsidies inevitably raise two questions: (1) are the beneficiary states in need of such help? (2) are they deserving of it? Table 5 provides data which help to answer these questions. All the numbers in Table 5 are relative, showing the ranking of each state according to various criteria. Thus Alabama ranks seventeenth according to the amount of subsidy received, twentieth according to the size of the required tax, 23.5 (tied with Tennessee) according to the level of unemployment, forty-ninth in per capita income, and forty-fourth in its tax effort (tax/benefit ratio).

Column 1 of Table 5 shows the states ranked according to the amount of subsidy that they would receive. In column 2 they are ranked according to the amount of subsidy divided by the covered payroll of each state. Thus the factor of state size is removed from the comparisons, and for most purposes column 2 provides the more useful ranking. The principal purpose of Table 5 is to permit a comparison between rankings in column 2 with those in the remaining four columns.

Columns 3, 4, and 5 throw some light on the issue of need, while column 6 relates to the issue of merit. The plus sign at the head of columns 3, 4, and 6 is a reminder that the correlation between these columns and column 2 should be positive. That is, smaller numbers in column 2 should be correlated with smaller numbers in columns 3, 4, and 6. In column 5, marked by a minus or negative sign, the opposite relation holds: smaller numbers in column 2 should correlate with larger numbers in column 5.

Relative Need for Subsidy

Other things being equal, we should expect that, under the Brodhead and Javits bills, unemployment insurance subsidies would be allocated in proportion to each state's need. One measure of need is the size of the prospective unemployment insurance tax burden in each state. Column 3 of Table 5 shows the states ranked according to the average tax each state would

Table 5
Ranking of States by Selected Criteria

State	Subsidy Absolute amount (1)	Subsidy Relative amount (2)	Future Tax Required (3) +	Average Unemployment (4) +	Per Capita Income (5) −	Tax/ Benefit Ratio (6) +
Alabama	17	17	20	23.5	49	44
Alaska	23	4	8.5	5	1	1.5
Arizona	22	14.5	28.5	19	32	40
Arkansas	25	12.5	16.5	15	50	20.5
California	2	19	16.5	14	10	8
Colorado	52[a]	52[a]	47	48.5	16	31.5
Connecticut	8	6	2	11	3	48
Delaware	33	27	16.5	27.5	5	28
District of Columbia	52[a]	52[a]	20	42	2	51
Florida	14	28	39.5	36	28	37.5
Georgia	19	26	41.5	37	37	37.5
Hawaii	35	35	12.5	18	9	16
Idaho	36	34	33	20	35	5
Illinois	6	13	22.5	25.5	6	49.5
Indiana	20	31	43.5	41	25	23
Iowa	52[a]	52[a]	39.5	46	20	34
Kansas	52[a]	52[a]	45	47	15	4
Kentucky	24	24	25	29	44	14
Louisiana	52[a]	52[a]	33	39	46	6
Maine	27	9	10	9	43	18
Maryland	26	29.5	22.5	33	11	47
Massachusetts	7	10	6	7.5	13	19
Michigan	1	2	7	4	12	34
Minnesota	52[a]	52[a]	20	35	23	25
Mississippi	29	32	47	40	31	7
Missouri	15	25	33	30	29	37.5
Montana	34	29.5	12.5	17	34	28
Nebraska	52[a]	52[a]	43.5	45	22	12
Nevada	28	21.5	11	16	7	9.5
New Hampshire	30	21.5	33	25.5	33	28
New Jersey	5	5	3	7.5	4	23
New Mexico	37	36	37	22	47	11
New York	4	16	14	13	8	28
North Carolina	9	11	37	32	39	44
North Dakota	52[a]	52[a]	28.5	44	35	3
Ohio	52[a]	52[a]	28.5	38	17	44
Oklahoma	52[a]	52[a]	41.5	43	36	14
Oregon	21	18	16.5	10	26	14
Pennsylvania	3	7	8.5	12	18	46
Puerto Rico	11	1	NA	1	52	20.5
Rhode Island	18	3	1	3	21	37.5
South Carolina	13	8	25	21	48	34
South Dakota	52[a]	52[a]	49.5	48.5	40	28
Tennessee	16	23	37	23.5	42	9.5
Texas	52[a]	52[a]	51	52	31	41.5
Utah	52[a]	52[a]	28.5	34	41	17
Vermont	31	12.5	4	6	38	49.5
Virginia	52[a]	52[a]	47	50	24	52

Table 5 (continued)

State	Subsidy		Future Tax Re-quired (3) +	Average Unem-ploy-ment (4) +	Per Capita Income (5) −	Tax/ Benefit Ratio (6) +
	Absolute amount (1)	Relative amount (2)				
Washington	10	14.5	5	2	14	28
West Virginia	32	33	33	31	45	41.5
Wisconsin	12	20	25	27.5	27	23
Wyoming	52[a]	52[a]	49.5	51	19	1.5

NA: Not available.

[a] Zero subsidy.

Note: A plus sign indicates that numbers in the column should have a positive correlation with numbers in column 2; a minus sign indicates that a negative correlation should be expected.

Source: Absolute amount from Table 4, column 1; relative amount is absolute amount as a percentage of total payroll; future tax required from table 1; average unemployment is the average insured unemployment rate, 1974–1976, from Unemployment Insurance Service, U.S. Department of Labor; per capita income from U.S. Department of Commerce; tax/benefit ratio from Table 6, column 3.

have to levy on its employers in order to restore the state unemployment insurance trust fund to solvency by 1982. We should expect the rankings in column 3 to be generally similar to the rankings in column 2.

The smaller the difference between the two rankings, the better the correlation is between the projected subsidy and the need for subsidy. A negative difference (column 2 less than column 3) indicates a subsidy greater than need, while a positive difference (column 2 greater than column 3) indicates a subsidy smaller than need. In both cases, of course, the norm is relative to other states. Large differences between numbers in columns 2 and 3 indicate that the proposed subsidy system is not achieving its objective, if judged by need.

Fifteen states show a difference between columns 2 and 3 of ten (9.5 rounded to 10) or more.[9] Of these, only two show a difference as large as 20: Hawaii with 22.5 would be the most undersubsidized state and North Carolina with a minus 26 would be the most oversubsidized state. Of the fifteen, five involve undersubsidy, and ten involve oversubsidy. On the whole, the proposed system of subsidies would seem to attain its objective reasonably well by giving the most aid to those states that have the most need.

The major reason for the differences in numerical rankings among the states in column 3 (future tax required) is their different experiences with unemployment. It is not surprising, therefore, that these rankings are generally similar to those in column 4 (average unemployment). The difference in unemployment experience is the most basic reason why a program of cost equalization may be desirable. When need for a subsidy is measured by a state's history of unemployment (column 4), the correlation between subsidy and need is even closer than when need is measured by the future tax required (column 3). A difference of ten or more between column 2 and column 4 occurs in only nine states.[10] Of the nine, five are positive in sign (undersubsidized), four negative (oversubsidized). Again, Hawaii (17) and North Carolina (−21) show the largest differences. The rankings in column 4 (average unemployment) bear out the general conclusion reached in the analysis of column 3 (future tax required) that the proposed program of subsidies should correlate reasonably well with the needs of the states.

A third measure of need is provided in column 5, which ranks the states according to their average per capita income for the period 1970–1976. Per capita income is used here as a rough indication of a state's fiscal strength, that is, its capacity for self-help.

Ideally, the ranking of a state by subsidy should have the same relation to the median as its ranking by income, but in reverse order. That is, a state's ranking by subsidy should be as many places above the median as its income ranking is below the median. Puerto Rico and Maine illustrate this point. Puerto Rico ranks last (26 below the median) by income and first (26 above the median) by subsidy; Maine ranks 43 (17 below the median) in income and 9 (17 above the median) in subsidy. Connecticut, on the other hand, is oversubsidized. Ranking 3 (23 above the median) in income, it should rank 49 (23 below the median) in subsidy; instead it ranks 6 in subsidy, or 43 places too high. Louisiana exemplifies the undersubsidized situation. It ranks 46 (20 below the median) in income and should rank 6 (20 above the median) in subsidy; instead it ranks 52 in subsidy, or 46 places too low.

The most oversubsidized states (relatively speaking) are listed here. (The number in parentheses indicates the number of ranks by which a state's subsidy exceeds its "proper" rank.) Alaska (47), Connecticut (43), New Jersey (43), Michigan (38), Illinois (33), Massachusetts (29), New York (28), Rhode Island (28), Pennsylvania (27), Washington (23.5), Nevada (23.5), California (23).

The most undersubsidized states are: Louisiana (46), Utah (41), South Dakota (40), Oklahoma (36), North Dakota (35), New Mexico (31), Texas (31), West Virginia (26), Virginia (24), District of Columbia (24), Minnesota (23), Nebraska (22).

Obviously, the industrialized states have both the most unemployment and the most income. Although they carry the heaviest burden, they seem to have the most resources. The inevitable question is whether they should be subsidized. The data in column 5 do not, of course, constitute an adequate answer to that question. Other factors besides income need to be weighed in determining the relative ability of a state to bear a given tax burden. Column 5 mainly raises the question and serves as a reminder that the question has not been answered by the bills' proponents, on whom the burden of proof rests.

Relative Tax Effort

Another factor helping to explain the differences in future tax burdens is the relative tax effort put forth by the various states in the past. If two states with the same unemployment experience are compared, the one that put forth the greater tax effort in the past should have the smaller tax burden in the future. Column 6 ranks the states by their tax effort over the period 1970–1976 as measured by the average ratio of taxes to benefits. The desired correlation is positive. That is, the larger the subsidy received by a state, the higher it should rank in its history of tax effort. The most undesirable situation would be ranking of first in subsidy and last in tax effort. In general, the smaller the difference in the two rankings, the better the situation.

A state may be considered to deserve the subsidy it receives if its ranking by tax effort (column 5) is the same, or close to the same, as its ranking by subsidy received (column 2). The larger the negative difference between the two rankings (subsidy ranking numerically lower than tax effort ranking) the greater is the "undeserved" subsidy. A positive difference (subsidy ranking numerically greater than tax effort ranking) has the opposite meaning: the state "deserves" a larger subsidy than it receives—always relative to other states.

The two midwestern states of Kansas and Illinois illustrate the contrasting situations. Since Kansas would receive no subsidy it ranks 52 by subsidy received, but it ranks 4 by tax effort—a positive difference of 48. Illinois, by contrast, ranks 13 according to subsidy received but only 49.5 according to tax effort—a negative difference of 36.5. During the years that Kansas was taxing its employers at an average rate of 0.92 percent, Illinois was content to levy a tax of only 0.54 percent (Table 6, column 2). Thus, by the norm of tax effort, Illinois' "right" to receive a subsidy of $316 million (Table 4, column 1) is debatable. The comparison of columns 2 and 5 reveals that twenty states have negative differences of 10 or more. Indeed, seven states show negative differences of 30 or more: Connecticut, Illinois, Michigan, North Carolina, Pennsylvania, Rhode Island, and Vermont.

The rankings in column 6 are based on the data in Table 6, which is significant in its own right. Table 6 shows the average tax rate that each state levied on its employers (column 2) during the seven-year period 1970–1976. It also shows each state's benefit-cost rate (column 1) during that same period. The ratio of taxes to benefits (column 3) provides a measure

Table 6
Measures of Tax Effort by State,
Averages of Period 1970–1976, and 1977 Tax Rate

	Average Benefit-Cost Rate[a] (1)	Average Tax Rate[b] (2)	Tax/Benefit Ratio (2) ÷ (1) (3)	1977 Tax Rate[b] (estimated) (4)
United States	1.22	0.89	0.73	1.3
Alabama	1.05	0.69	0.66	1.0
Alaska	1.67	2.22	1.33	1.9
Arizona	0.95	0.65	0.68	1.3
Arkansas	1.18	0.88	0.75	1.3
California	1.52	1.37	0.90	1.9
Colorado	0.56	0.40	0.71	1.2
Connecticut	2.03	1.16	0.57	1.5
Delaware	1.25	0.90	0.72	1.0
District of Columbia	1.08	0.53	0.49	1.0
Florida	0.68	0.47	0.69	1.3
Georgia	0.78	0.54	0.69	1.0
Hawaii	1.64	1.31	0.80	2.4
Idaho	1.14	1.09	0.96	1.5
Illinois	1.03	0.54	0.52	1.2
Indiana	0.72	0.53	0.74	0.8
Iowa	0.86	0.60	0.70	1.4
Kansas	0.86	0.92	1.07	1.0
Kentucky	1.08	0.87	0.81	1.3
Louisiana	1.00	0.92	0.92	1.0
Maine	1.70	1.33	0.78	1.6
Maryland	1.07	0.63	0.59	1.4
Massachusetts	1.91	1.47	0.77	1.7
Michigan	1.52	1.06	0.70	1.8
Minnesota	1.06	0.77	0.73	1.4
Mississippi	0.66	0.60	0.91	1.2
Missouri	0.98	0.68	0.69	1.1
Montana	1.25	0.90	0.72	1.6
Nebraska	0.77	0.64	0.83	0.8
Nevada	1.64	1.40	0.85	1.9
New Hampshire	1.05	0.76	0.72	0.9
New Jersey	2.00	1.47	0.74	2.0
New Mexico	1.00	0.84	0.84	1.0
New York	1.46	1.05	0.72	1.3
North Carolina	0.88	0.58	0.66	0.9
North Dakota	1.04	1.13	1.09	1.5
Ohio	0.88	0.58	0.66	1.0
Oklahoma	0.74	0.60	0.81	1.0
Oregon	1.36	1.10	0.81	2.1
Pennsylvania	1.62	0.97	0.60	1.3
Puerto Rico	2.85	2.15	0.75	NA
Rhode Island	2.25	1.55	0.69	1.9
South Carolina	1.02	0.71	0.70	1.1
South Dakota	0.61	0.44	0.72	0.5
Tennessee	0.93	0.79	0.85	0.9
Texas	0.36	0.24	0.67	0.4
Utah	1.06	0.84	0.79	1.3
Vermont	1.85	0.96	0.52	2.2
Virginia	0.50	0.24	0.48	1.1

Table 6 (continued)

	Average Benefit-Cost Rate[a] (1)	Average Tax Rate[b] (2)	Tax/Benefit Ratio (2) ÷ (1) (3)	1977 Tax Rate[b] (estimated) (4)
Washington	2.10	1.49	0.71	1.8
West Virginia	0.85	0.57	0.67	0.9
Wisconsin	1.19	0.88	0.74	2.4
Wyoming	0.52	0.69	1.33	1.0

[a] Benefits as percent of total payrolls.
[b] Taxes as percent of total payrolls.
Source: U.S. Department of Labor, Employment and Training Administration, Unemployment Insurance Service, October 1977.

of tax effort in response to benefit experience. Finally, the table shows the tax rate levied by each state in 1977 (column 4).

The ten states which would receive 79 percent of the total subsidies (see footnote 6) do not include a single state that had levied an average tax on its employers as high as 1.5 percent of total wages. None except California had maintained a ratio of taxes to benefits as high as .80. Of these ten states, Connecticut, Illinois, North Carolina, and Pennsylvania had particularly low tax/benefit ratios. Three had taxed their employers at an average rate of less than 1 percent: Illinois (0.54 percent), North Carolina (0.66 percent), and Pennsylvania (0.97 percent).

It will be recalled from Table 1 that five states (Connecticut, New Jersey, Rhode Island, Vermont, and Washington) faced the heaviest future tax burdens. These states would have to tax their employers at an average rate of 3 percent or more (of total wages) during the five-year period 1978–1982 to restore adequate reserves to their unemployment insurance trust funds. Of these states, only Rhode Island has taxed its employers as much as 1.5 percent (on the average) during the preceding seven years (1970–1976). Only two of these five states had responded to the crisis and raised their average tax rate as high as 2 percent by 1977: New Jersey (2.0 percent) and Vermont (2.2 percent). States which show a low measure of tax effort have the burden of showing that they should receive the relief that the bills would provide.

Supporting Arguments for the Bills

States Not Responsible for Unemployment. Our society has a tradition of helping members that are experiencing unusual difficulty. A common example is the aid that the federal government provides to disaster areas. It is claimed that states that are burdened by unusually high unemployment should qualify for appropriate assistance because unemployment, like a natural disaster,

35

is beyond the control of the states. The state of Washington because of its climate and its seasonal industries has more unemployment than the state of Texas. No matter how hard it tried, Washington could not bring its unemployment rate down to the low level that Texas enjoys. Even adjoining states like Michigan and Ohio have very different unemployment rates (Michigan high, Ohio low) because of their different industrial activities. It is in the nature of the auto industry, for example, to have above average unemployment because of fluctuating demand. It is therefore claimed that consumers should bear part of the cost of that unemployment. A state which serves as the home for automobile manufacturers should not be burdened with the entire cost of unemployment in that industry.

The burden of cyclical unemployment should not be left to states which happen to experience more of it, it is argued, for two reasons. First, cyclical unemployment is not predictable, and the individual states should not be required to build up adequate reserves against such a threat. Second, the business cycle is, by definition, a broad, national phenomenon resulting from national causes outside the control of the individual states. Unemployment benefits for cyclical unemployment, it is contended, should be paid for, at least in part, by a tax levied on the entire economy. The burden should not be borne by only a few states.

State Competition. For some years now there has been a flow of industry into the sun belt states at the expense of the snow belt states. It is argued that this flow should not be permitted to proceed so fast that great economic losses are sustained as factories and utilities are left to deteriorate in the North while new ones are built in the South. If the unemployment insurance bills would provide more help to the North than the South, as they probably would, this assistance might slow the pace of the exodus to the South. Although the amount of assistance provided would be small, when the margin of profit is thin, as it is for the industries involved, "every little bit helps."

Although the states in the North would probably receive a disproportionate part of the subsidy, they are the ones that pay a proportionately larger share of federal taxes. The present pattern of federal taxes and benefits still reflects the former and now rapidly changing pattern of income distribution through which the North subsidizes the South. The subsidy provided by the proposed program would represent only a slight correction of the existing imbalance.

Opposition Arguments

Responsibility for Unemployment. Economic losses sustained in the regular course of doing business normally are not borne by government. Unemployment insurance costs, it is claimed, are among the regular costs of doing business. They are about as predictable as most other business costs, and they are as traceable to particular economic conditions as are other costs of doing business. In these respects unemployment differs from what are termed natural disasters. A firm engaged in outside construction work expects to experience more unemployment than one engaged in inside construction, and very much more than a firm engaged in banking. These differential costs get translated into differential prices of various kinds by the normal workings of the competitive market.

The word "responsible" can be ambiguous. When it is said that a firm is responsible for its own unemployment, this need not mean that the firm is at fault or that the firm or state could or should have done something different to prevent unemployment. The firm may be responsible for the unemployment only in the sense that the costs of unemployment benefits are a regular, predictable cost of engaging in the kind of economic activity followed by the firm. Like other business costs, unemployment insurance costs are assigned to their source and thus become a part of the price mechanism which is the principal method employed to allocate resources in our society. Whether the employer could have avoided the unemployment is unrelated to this meaning of responsibility.

It is claimed that cyclical unemployment does not differ substantially from other kinds of unemployment. Some economic activities are known to be more cyclically sensitive than others, and this characteristic normally enters into the cost calculations of firms which engage in such activities. Although somewhat less predictable than other kinds of unemployment and somewhat larger in amount, cyclical unemployment, it is argued, clearly belongs among the regular costs of doing business.

The argument that cyclical unemployment is different from other unemployment because it flows from "national causes" is misleading. Any and every kind of unemployment can come from "national causes." The cyclically unemployed are no different from the unemployed in general, and their unemployment stems from the same personal and impersonal causes. A business recession is merely a time when these causes are more operative than usual, that is, when a greater number of firms than usual are cutting back on economic activity. As noted above, some economic activities are known to be more cyclically sensitive than others, and a firm engaged in them normally takes this characteristic into account in its pricing policies. The cost of unemployment benefits is only a part, a very small part, of the costs that an employer expects to meet because of cyclical conditions. (The issue, it should be remembered, is not the payment of unemployment benefits—this is to be done in any case—but only the allocation of the costs of such benefits.)

While it can be admitted, for the sake of argument, that people in Texas who wish to use automobiles manufactured in Michigan should be ready to share in the cost of the unemployment benefits necessarily connected with the production of automobiles, it does not follow that the best way to achieve this sharing is by having the employers or taxpayers of Texas pay a subsidy to the employers of Michigan. The normal method of cost sharing is for the manufacturer to include its costs of unemployment insurance in the price of its automobiles. This price is paid only by those who purchase that make of automobile, the normal way that costs and resources are allocated in a market economy.

Should the cost of unemployment benefits for a particular state or industry become so large that an unusual and unexpected burden is placed on a state or industry, this problem can be met by borrowing from the federal unemployment account as at present. Relief beyond this should require clear evidence that the taxes required to meet costs would be "unbearable." The bills under discussion propose the norm of 6 percent insured unemployment as the point at which unemployment costs become unbearable and thus justify subsidies from a central fund. Opponents claim that no evidence has been presented which establishes that a 6 percent unemployment rate is unbearable. But on the contrary, there is evidence that casts doubt on this assumption. For example, the state of Washington has had an average insured unemployment rate of over 8 percent during the past seven years and yet has managed to stay afloat and administer a respectable unemployment insurance program. Evidence is needed that other states cannot do the same.

When the unemployment insurance program was first established in 1935, a decision was made that, given the weak state of the economy at that time, the maximum tax rate should not exceed 3 percent of total wages. Since the economy is much stronger today than it was then, the question inevitably arises, why firms today are unable to meet a tax rate above 2 percent of total wages (the cost equivalent of a 6 percent insured unemployment rate). Although it can be said that there was no basis for the earlier estimate of a 3 percent maximum tax rate, it may be said with equal truth that no evidence has been offered that states are unable to levy a tax higher than 2 percent.

Competition among the States. Although the income gap between North and South is narrowing, the northern states are still richer than those of the South. Therefore, it is argued, the richer states should meet their own unemployment insurance costs. There is not the same justification for subsidizing the North today as there was for subsidizing the South in an earlier generation. Instead, it is asserted that we seem to be approaching a more balanced situation in which each state may properly be required to meet its own costs.

The argument that the unemployment insurance tax has a significant effect on the movement of firms into or out of a state has often been advanced but has never been supported by concrete evidence. In fact, the available evidence runs counter to this proposition. The unemployment insurance tax is a small part of fringe benefits, a much smaller part of employee remuneration, and a still smaller part of total production costs. Business leaders who have testified before Congress have all taken the position that the unemployment tax ranks far down the list of factors that influence an employer's choice of location.

To the argument that a change in the unemployment insurance tax can be significant to the well-being of an employer with a small profit margin, and that in states where industrial activity is declining there may be many such employers, it is responded that the cost of supporting unemployed workers is a regular cost of doing business and that the cost should be permitted to have its influence on the conduct of the employer. Only when all costs are faithfully reflected in prices will the price system and the competitive market system work best. Rather than continue to subsidize weak industries, it is better in the long run to let industries which cannot pay their own costs change to other product lines or move or go out of business. A final argument is that subsidizing inefficient operations also adds to inflation, our number one domestic problem.

IMPACT ON THE NATIONAL ECONOMY

Arguments based on the impact of pending bills on the national economy carry less weight than those which deal with the bills' effect on the unemployment insurance program (which would be major) and their effect on the economies of individual states. The impact on the national economy would be smaller, in relative terms, because the amounts are not large when compared with the total national economy and because of uncertainty as to how the federal contributions would be financed. If additional taxes were levied, it is not known which taxes would be raised or whether increased federal contributions would be financed through a larger deficit in the federal budget, that is, through federal borrowing.

Arguments Favoring the Bills

Proponents of the pending legislation argue that since there is a close interrelation between economic units in the complex modern economy, there is always the danger that weakness in a few units will spread to others and gradually slow down the whole economy. It is wise to have a preventive program that automatically provides assistance to a state whose rising unemployment rate signals an economic virus.

Since payroll taxes for unemployment insurance raise the cost of hiring workers, they act as a brake on hiring. The substitution of general revenues for a payroll tax removes this direct obstacle to growth in employment. If the general revenues are derived not from an increased tax but from deficit financing, it is argued that this will replace lost purchasing power and supply a needed stimulus for the general economy.

Arguments Against the Bills

Opponents contend that the analogy of the spread of a viral infection is misplaced when used in the context of the unemployment insurance program. The revenues from the unemployment insurance tax are a very small part of a state's budget. The aid that a state might receive from enactment of the bills under consideration is too small to have a significant effect on the general economic health of the state. If a state's employers cannot support themselves and pay the small tax involved, they are in need of a more basic remedy than the subsidy offered by these bills. The general economy is generally not helped by protecting economic activities that cannot pay their way.

Replacing a payroll tax with general revenues would remove some of the incentive employers now have to minimize the unemployment connected with their operations. In the long run, this might weaken the general economy. If, in addition, taxes do not cover the cost, more deficit financing might lead to more inflation and a less sound economy in the long run.

NOTES TO TEXT

[1] The statutory provisions governing the unemployment insurance program are contained in 42 U.S.C. 501-504 (grants to states for administration), 42 U.S.C. 1101-1108 (administering the financing of the program), and 26 U.S.C. 3301-3311 (unemployment insurance taxes). Special provision regarding federal employees and certain ex-service personnel may be found at 5 U.S.C. 8501-8525. Railroad unemployment insurance is covered at 45 U.S.C. 351-403. Financing for these programs is provided by the federal government and will not be dealt with in this analysis.

[2] H.R. 8292 was introduced on July 13, 1977, and referred to the Ways and Means Committee which has referred consideration to the Subcommittee on Public Assistance and Unemployment Compensation. S. 1853 was introduced July 13, 1977, and referred to the Senate Finance Committee. S. 1853 has three titles. Only the first is analyzed here. The second title deals with the duration of benefits and hence lies outside the area of financing as such. The bill's third title proposes norms for the rate at which states should repay debts owed to the federal treasury. Although this is a financing issue, this analysis is concerned only with the distribution of the tax burden through a permanent program of reinsurance and cost equalization.

[3] The federal unemployment tax rate was increased from 3.2 to 3.4 percent effective January 1, 1977, by Public Law 94-566, which extended the coverage of the unemployment insurance program to many additional employees and expanded the taxable wage base from $4,200 to $6,000 effective January 1, 1978. The tax rate will revert to 3.2 percent when all of the repayable advances to the extended unemployment compensation account in the federal unemployment trust fund are repaid. (The administration's 1978 tax proposal calls for the reduction of the federal tax rate to 3.2 percent of the taxable wages effective December 31, 1978. See section 421 of H.R. 12078, 95th Congress, 2d session.) A state may supersede up to 2.7 percent of this tax, thus reducing the federal "take" to the difference between the federal tax and 2.7 percent. The original difference was 0.3 percent, less than half the current 0.7 percent.

[4] The extended benefits program was established by Public Law 91-373 to pay additional benefits to workers who have exhausted their entitlement to the basic maximum of twenty-six weeks of regular benefits during periods of high unemployment. Triggered by a designated unemployment rate in the state or in the nation, benefit payments could be stretched out to a maximum of thirty-nine weeks, with extended payments financed equally by the state and federal governments. Public Law 93-572 authorized emergency benefits under the federal supplemental benefits program for workers in states with high unemployment rates who had exhausted their right to both regular and extended benefits. The cost of emergency benefits (covering a maximum of thirteen additional weeks), paid after March 1977 are

met from general revenues. Before that date these supplemental benefits were financed by a uniform federal tax levied on all employers nationwide. At one point during the last recession, this program permitted payments for up to sixty-five weeks. This emergency program was terminated by Congress in the fall of 1977, and the last supplemental benefits were paid early in 1978.

[5] The adequate level is defined as one that is 1.5 times the highest annual amount paid out by the state during the most recent ten years. This is a rough measure, the reliability of which varies from state to state.

[6] There is no interstate sharing of the cost of regular benefits or of a state's portion of extended benefits. Similarly, the flow of funds from the federal unemployment account to state trust funds has no element of sharing in it. These loans are repayable in full by the borrowing states (Table 2).

Extended unemployment compensation account expenditures (Figure 1) are shared, however. These funds, which finance the federal share (that is, half of extended benefits and all supplementary benefits) come from a uniform tax on the employers of all states, but the funds are distributed to states in proportion to the amount of long-term unemployment in each. Since unemployment varies greatly among states (see Figure 3), the mechanism of the extended unemployment compensation account results in the employers of some states subsidizing employers in other states.

The bills under consideration propose to change the system by drawing on general revenues for some of the costs of benefits paid by states in their regular and extended unemployment insurance programs. The proposed change may be shown graphically by drawing a line from the box "general revenue" in Figure 1 to the top two boxes on the right of the chart. This line should be titled "nonrepayable advances." The effect of the change would be to require the general taxpayer to bear part of the cost of unemployment benefits in some states. It would probably also require some states to subsidize other states on a somewhat predictable basis.

(Congress has provided for the payment of federal supplemental benefits subsequent to March 1977 to be made out of nonrepayable advances from general revenues. This may be shown in Figure 1 by a line running from the box "general revenues" to the box on the right marked "100 percent federal supplemental benefits.")

[7] One attempt to test this correlation found that, of four measures of liberality, two had no correlation at all with high and low costs. The two that did correlate were correlated negatively—that is, the states with the higher costs had the more liberal programs. See Joseph M. Becker, *Experience Rating in Unemployment Insurance: An Experiment in Competitive Socialism* (Baltimore: Johns Hopkins University Press, 1972), pp. 214 and 364.

[8] California, Connecticut, Illinois, Massachusetts, Michigan, New Jersey, New York, North Carolina, Pennsylvania, and Washington.

[9] Arizona, Delaware, Florida, Georgia, Hawaii, Illinois, Indiana, Mississippi, Montana, Nevada, New Hampshire, North Carolina, South Carolina, Tennessee, and Washington.

[10] Hawaii, Idaho, Illinois, Indiana, Montana, New Mexico, North Carolina, South Carolina, and Washington.